Time Pieces for Guitar
Volume 2

c.1250   Sumer is icumen in

Anon.

This arrangement imagines how the melody of one of the earliest known rounds might have sounded as an instrumental.

AB 3412

*c.*1380 Saltarello

Anon.

A saltarello ('little hop' in Italian) was a moderately quick jumping dance in triple time.

AB 3412

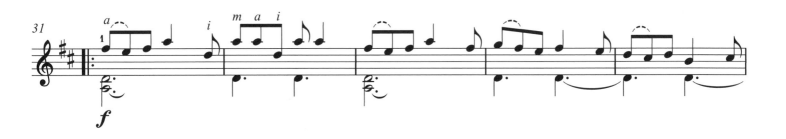

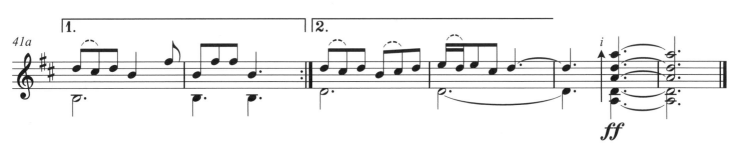

1552 Two Branles

from *Le premier livre...de guiterne*

Guillaume Morlaye
(*c.1510–c.1565*)

No. 1

No. 2

The branle (or 'brawl') was a dance in which men and women held hands and stepped together, often in a circle. *Le premier livre… de guiterne* was one of the earliest books of music for the four-course guitar.

1597   **Two Pieces**

John Dowland
(1563–1626)

Now, O now I needs must part

This tune is from *The First Booke of Songes or Ayres*. Dowland later turned it into a lute solo called *The Frog Galliard*.

Tarleton's Resurrection

Richard Tarleton was a famous Elizabethan clown who acted in William Shakespeare's company.

1613   Never weather-beaten sail

Thomas Campion
(1567–1620)

1663   Italian Rant

Anon.

from *Musicks Hand-Maide*

1692 Rondeau

from *The Fairy Queen*

Henry Purcell
(1659–1695)

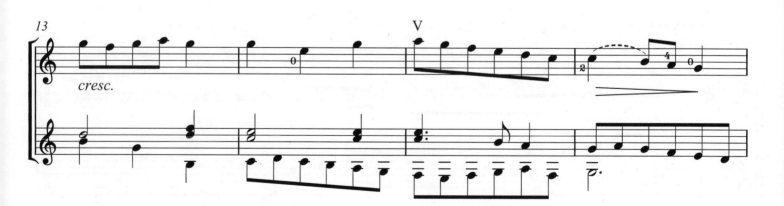

D.C. al Fine

1709   Three Pieces

George Frideric Handel
(1685–1759)

Gavotte

Bourrée

D.C. al Fine

Gigue

These contemporaneous settings of Handel are from 'Lord Danby's Lute Book', a collection featuring several composers. It was compiled by William Osborne, who lived in Hamburg between 1706 and 1711, a few years after the composer. The Gigue is from *Almira*, Handel's first opera.

*c.*1720 Musette

from *English Suite No. 3*

Johann Sebastian Bach
(1685–1750)

AB 3412

1725 Largo

Antonio Vivaldi
(1678–1741)

from 'Winter', *The Four Seasons*

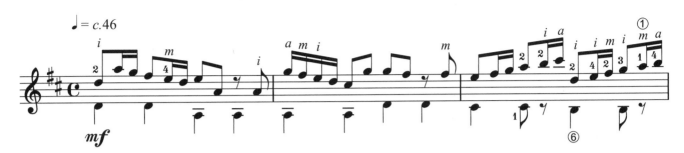

Menuet

from *Nouvelles suites de pièces de clavecin*

Jean-Philippe Rameau
(1683–1764)

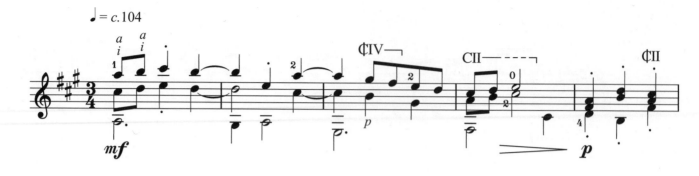

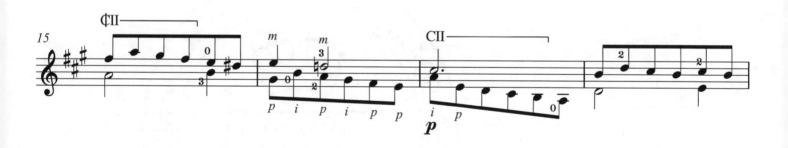

1762 Allegro

K. 3

Wolfgang Amadeus Mozart
(1756–1791)

1763 Menuet

Hob. IX/3 No. 2

Joseph Haydn
(1732–1809)

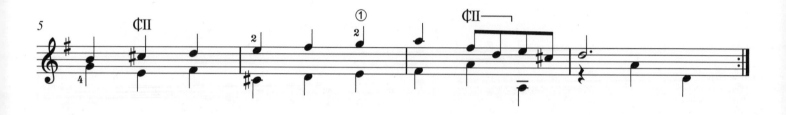

AB 3412

1787 **The Ploughboy**

from *The Farmer*

William Shield
(1748–1829)

*c.*1790 Moderato

from Sonatina in G (Anh. 5/1)

attrib. Ludwig van Beethoven
(1770–1827)

AB 3412

1815 Allegretto

Op. 50 No. 15

Mauro Giuliani
(1781–1829)

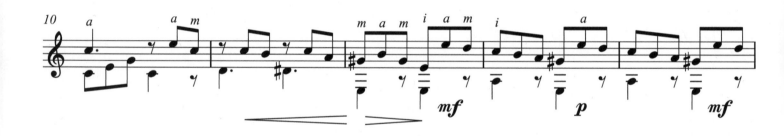

AB 3412

c.1828 Pastorale

Op. 21 No. 16

Matteo Carcassi
(1792–1853)

Andante ♩ = c.100

AB 3412

c.1847 Three Pieces
from *Schule für die Guitare*

Johann Kaspar Mertz
(1806–1856)

No. 1

No. 2

AB 3412

No. 3

1872 Funeral March of a Marionette

Charles-François Gounod
(1818–1893)

AB 3412

1878   March of the Wooden Soldiers

Pyotr Tchaikovsky
(1840–1893)

from *Album for the Young*

Tempo di marcia ♩ = *c.*96

AB 3412

1887   Vals poético No. 1

Enrique Granados
(1867–1916)

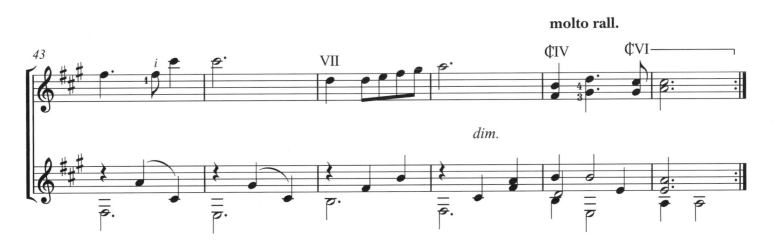

*c.*1900   Prelude 'Lágrima'

Francisco Tárrega
(1852–1909)

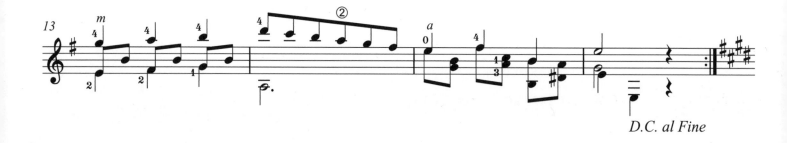

Lágrima   Teardrop

Two Lessons

*c.*1910

from *Método para guitarra*

José Ferrer
(1835–1916)

Lección 16

Source: the Robert Spencer Collection at the Royal Academy of Music Library (Ms611), London

Lección 24

1926 Bye Bye Blackbird

Ray Henderson (1896–1970)
Words by Mort Dixon

Smooth, with lightly swung quavers ♩ = *c.*132

AB 3412

c.1930 No walk today!

from *Children's Album*, book 1

Aram Khachaturian
(1903–1978)

AB 3412

1940 Hop-Scotch

from *Duets for Children*

William Walton
(1902–1983)

AB 3412

1959 My Favorite Things

1959

from *The Sound of Music*

Richard Rodgers (1902–1979)
Words by Oscar Hammerstein II

1969   So long, Frank Lloyd Wright

Paul Simon
(b. 1941)

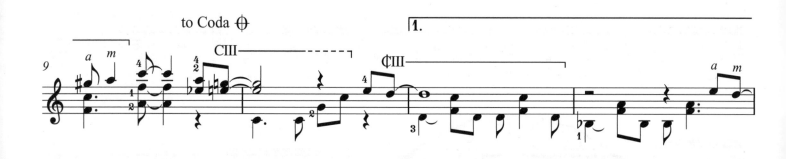

This song is from Simon and Garfunkel's best-selling album, *Bridge Over Troubled Water*.

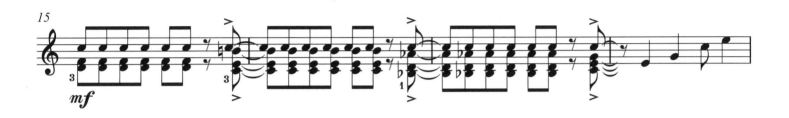

D.C. al Coda

1982   Senhorinha

Guinga
(b. 1950)

Guinga (real name Carlos Althier de Souza Lemos Escobar) is a popular Brazilian songwriter. 'Senhorinha', his best-known song, was composed as a lullaby for his young daughters.

2005   **The Acrobat**

Peter Wrieden
(b. 1972)

2006   I Spy

Colin Downs
(b. 1949)

Japanese Water Garden

2007

Stephen Goss
(b. 1964)

Music origination by Andrew Jones
Printed in England by Caligraving Ltd, Thetford, Norfolk